BLACK PUNK
A Play in One Act
By Kenneth Grimes

Humboldt Street
Writers Group

Black Punk: A Play in One Act

Published by Bush League Books, in association with The Humboldt Street Writers Group

Copyright © 2024 The Estate of Kenneth Grimes

Original © 1989 Kenneth Grimes

All rights reserved. No portion of this book may be reproduced in any form without permission from the publisher, except as permitted by U.S. copyright law.

For permissions contact: heartcom2@msn.com

Cover Photo by Eugene Triguba on Unsplash. Used under irrevocable, nonexclusive, worldwide copyright license under Unsplash.

Ken Grimes portrait courtesy of the Estate of Kenneth Grimes. All rights reserved.

ISBN: 979-8-9917151-1-9

Printed in the United States of America

First Edition

Tribute to Ken

Ninawaalika Wababa wote na Wamama wote kushuhudia sherehe hiyo.

Swahili - "I invite all Fathers and Mothers to bear witness to this ceremony,"

an invocation to Ken's ancestors to honor and celebrate his accomplishments.

To Ken's family, and to his artistic and community families, thank you for giving me this honor. The opening line of a poem by Drew Chalker reads "People come into your life for a reason, a season, or a lifetime."

Ken and I met and began working together at the Denver Black Arts Company (DBAC), which began in 1976 and nurtured today's leaders in African-American theater. Ken became a key Black playwright, director and actor while working as a major community arts producer, activist and educator. An advocate for the importance of arts and culture for the health of his community, he shared his talents as Director of the Marcus Garvey Center at the University of Northern Colorado, as well as with youth and community leadership development in the Cooperative Extension Services of Colorado State University. A Man for All Seasons.... winter, spring, summer or fall.

Ken's canon of locally produced plays included "Passion Rhapsody" performed at Casino Cabaret; "Barca, Man of Lightning" performed at the Community House; and the adaptation of Margaree King Mitchell's book, "Uncle Jed's Barbershop," which played off-Broadway in New York and at

Cleo Parker Robinson's Dance Theater. He directed the very first play at the Donald Todd Theatre, "Wine in the Wilderness" by Alice Childress.

Coming from our work at DBAC, I co-founded Eulipions, Inc. in 1982, and Ken's strengths undergirded our subsequent key development of Eulipions Theatre Company. The majority of Eulipions' plays were directed by Ken. The most popular were "The Meeting" by Jeff Stetson, "Tambourines to Glory" by Langston Hughes, "Mahalia's Song" by Dr. Vada Butcher, and "Mama, I Want to Sing" by Vy Higgenson.

His final production at Eulipions was a play his Mother wrote about their family car, a play using the car as an analogy for family joys, challenges, break-downs, recovery, and mostly about the strength of love that keeps a family together. Because truly, Ken loved his family more than anything, his sons, his grandchildren, his great grandchildren and his extended adopted family. He was a father to many who did not have fathers, he was generous with his time, his wisdom and his care. You his family brought so much joy to him. I am grateful to you.

Yeah, yeah, yeah, yeah, yeah yeah yeah yeah, sang Pharoah Sanders. The Creator has a Master Plan, Peace and Happiness throughout the Land. Ken was a part of that Master Plan.

His physical being is no more, and I will miss especially his humor, his jokes, and the times we'd gather at our legendary local community restaurants: Goodfriends, Kapre Lounge, and Racine's. I will miss too our discussions coming from his being such a prolific reader, and our debates about the meanings of plays, films, books, characters, portrayals, and of course politics. Throughout our fifty years collaborating we would recommend all sorts of articles and works of literature to each other. We last discussed the TV series "Succession" which is supposedly based on MacBeth. Ken..."Really?" Lifetime friends are rare, and will often tell you just what you do not want to hear.

As Carole King sang, Winter, spring, summer or fall, all you have to do is call, and I'll be right there -- you've got a friend! The last line of the Chalker poem I quoted at the beginning is, "It is said that love is blind, but friendship, friendship is clairvoyant." Clairvoyant—the ability to see beyond differences, pettiness, disagreements, and to see the future possibilities and possibilities for a future.

His body is not here. Nevertheless, his spirit remains.

Asante!

Proverbs 17:17 — A friend loves at all times, and a brother is born for a time of adversity...a friend is always loyal, and a brother is born to help in time of need.

~ Jo Bunton Keel
Artist, Director, Producer, Educator... and Friend

Ken Grimes Artistic Biography

Kenneth Grimes (1949-2023), one of Colorado's most important creatives in recent decades, wrote award-winning musicals, dramatic plays, short stories, and poetry. His most recent musical, *Uncle Jed's Barbershop*, was a finalist for the O'Neill Musical Theatre Conference, a winner of the ASCAP Disney Award, and was selected as a Director's Choice Award and off-Broadway showcase for the New York Musical Theatre Festival. Ken's other musicals include *Barca: Man of Lightning* about the ancient Phoenician General, Hannibal; *Gifts: A Lesson in Giving*, a show written as a traveling production for the Denver Public Schools; and *Girlz*, which engaged youth and adults learning from each other in a gospel dramatization. His dramatic plays include *Reverend W. T. Liggins*; *Passion Rhapsody*; and *Ain't No Grave*, about the first female African American doctor in Colorado; *The Queen Must Die* and the previously unpublished *Black Punk*. Ken served as artistic director of the Denver Black Arts Company and as the long-term main director for Eulipions Cultural Center. Plays he directed include *Mahalia's Song* by Dr. Vada Butcher with a two-year run, and *Mama I Wanna Sing* by Vy Higginsen and Ken Wydro, also with a long run. A trained dramaturge, he served as President of Colorado Dramatists, having workshopped his plays with some of the country's most noted writers, including Peter Shaffer (*Amadeus*), August Wilson (*Fences*), and Stephen Schwartz (*Wicked*).

An Invitation

Black Punk, a previously unpublished play in one act by Kenneth Grimes, is a raw, unflinching short drama that rises from the ruins of young America's dreams of racial equality and harmony and lands center stage as a masterfully assembled blow to the heart.

Completed in 1989, the one-act play draws upon his explorations of the night-time culture of young people in the punk culture emerging in Philadelphia in the 1980s. *Black Punk* is a bootcamp for dealing with the feelings of the cultural breakup, disillusionment and grief its young characters find themselves in, post-Civil Rights, post-Black Power, and post-Vietnam. Coming through those eras, James Baldwin once observed that more than any other nation the United States disillusions its young, by shattering the dreams into which they've been raised.

These interracially connected characters take us on a fascinating and brutally verbalized journey through disillusion's aftermath. They lead us, with some small, merciful moments of the romantic, through vivid quests for what hits them, again and again, as impossible—reliable love and identity. Vigiling from the set's second floor, a woman of mystery never speaks and looks out across the audience. A maternal or madonna-like presence, she seems to be waiting for things not yet available to anyone onstage.

Bearing the fear and pity of classic tragedy, *Black Punk* arrives outfitted in twentieth century punk garb and language. It opens and closes with stark set-and-character images related to religious redemption and holds us close to the grief needed in healing our racial and cultural divides.

Ken Grimes' Life Context Through Black Punk (1989)

1949	Ken Grimes born in Denver; family moves to join relatives in Tulare, California.
1954	Family back to Denver; Supreme Court issues Brown vs. Board of Education ruling.
1955	Rosa Parks arrested; Montgomery bus boycott selects Rev. Martin Luther King, Jr. as head.
1957	Little Rock Nine children enter Central High School, later escorted by 101st Airborne.
1963	Southern Christian Leadership's Birmingham non-violent students defeat Bull Connor.
1963	SCLC leader Medgar Evers assassinated at his home in Mississippi.
1963	March on Washington, D.C.; Rev. Martin Luther King, Jr.'s "I Have a Dream" speech.
1963	President John F. Kennedy assassinated in Texas; Ken enters Denver's West High School.
1964	Cassius Clay wins world heavyweight title; changes name to Muhammad Ali.
1964	President Lyndon Baines Johnson signs the Civil Rights Act.
1964	Lyndon B. Johnson uses Gulf of Tonkin incident, expands U. S. military in Vietnam War.

1965	Malcolm X assassinated in Washington D.C.; book *Biography of Malcolm X* released.
1965	First Selma-to-Montgomery voting rights marchers brutalized in Selma.
1965	Lyndon B. Johnson signs the Voting Rights Act.
1965	Watts rebellion/riot in Los Angeles.
1966	SNCC officially opposes Black involvement in Vietnam War.
1966	Stokely Carmichael declares for Black Power movement.
1966	Black Panther party founded, Oakland, California.
1967	Rev. Martin Luther King, Jr.'s anti-Vietnam War speech, Riverside Church, New York City.
1967	Muhammad Ali refuses induction to Army for the Vietnam War.
1967	Ken graduates from West High School; college scholarship in track.
1967	Newark rebellion/riot in New Jersey.
1967	Detroit rebellion/riot; LBJ sends in 82nd and 101st Airborne Units.
1967	March on the Pentagon antiwar demonstration, D.C.
1968	Rev. Martin Luther King, Jr. assassinated during Memphis garbage workers strike.

1968	Holy Week Uprising rebellion/riot in D.C., Baltimore, Chicago, Kansas City, and other cities.
1968	Bobby Kennedy declares for presidency; assassinated in Los Angeles.
1968	Ken enters Colorado State University after one year of Community College; competes on track team.
1968	August Wilson presents *Recycling* in a local Pittsburgh theatre.
1968	Black U.S. sprinters give Black Power salute at the Mexico City Olympic Games.
1969	Trial of Chicago 7 includes Black Panther co-founder Bobby Seale, gagged during trial.
1969	Black Panther Fred Hampton, multiracial coalition builder, assassinated by Chicago Police.
1969	Woodstock Rock Festival attracts 500,000 attendees near Woodstock, New York.
1970	Ken meets and marries Gerie Grimes.
1970	Angela Davis becomes the third woman on FBI's most wanted list.
1971	Ken graduates from Colorado State University in English/Education.
c. 1973	Project New Pride, Denver, hires Ken as a teacher for youth offenders.
c. 1975	Punk music and cultural movement begins in London and New York.

1976	Denver Black Arts Company begins Black Theatre movement; Ken and Jo Bunton-Keel work with the company.
1982	Jo Bunton-Keel & Jimmy Walker found Eulipions, Black theatre's primary venue.
1985	August Wilson completes *Fences*.
c. 1985	Ken works in Philadelphia; experiences the growing punk culture.
1989	Ken completes *Black Punk*, inspired by Philadelphia's punk scene.

Creating Black Punk

Ken's childhood experience and upbringing kept him fascinated lifelong by the fine line young people come to walk who've grown up in not-so-privileged circumstances like his, while embodying tons of talent, intelligence, vibrant personalities and creative ingenuity. One pathway, as it emerged for him under the vigilance of his single mother, an aspirant writer raising her family of seven children in Denver's west side projects, trended into choices for constructive dreams and possibilities despite all challenges, and explorations into the so-called mainstream culture to open it, often despite itself, into a richer, fuller life for everybody. Another pathway, into which, not infrequently, Ken's vibrant young neighbors were drawn, trended into gradually growing social alienation and socioeconomic oppressions, often involving problems with legal systems, jailings and imprisonment. (See, in action, his vivid young characters reaching the age of choice at the point those two trends diverge, in Ken's short story "Oasis" and his incomplete novel "No Rats in My Gutter", featured exclusively in *An Anthology from Another Bunch of Writers You Never Heard Of: the Humboldt Street Writers Group in Action,* companion collection to *Black Punk.*)

Ken's ancillary work, complementing his theatre and literary accomplishments, was the life-long teaching and organizing of program opportunities to empower the dreams of such vivid young center-city youth with leadership and life skills, urging them to develop joy-giving practical steps to enliven their own, their families' and their communities' lives by creating work and social options, to flourish into pride, happiness, and healthy relationships. He began work in Denver's national-modeling New Pride non-resident diversion program for multi-felony youth offenders shortly after it began in 1973. It brought him daily to that work, to reopen the first of the two pathways above for the kind of young people he'd grown up with, many pulled early and deeply into that second disempowering trend that left them feeling they had little or no future in our shared society.

Ken's job following his years at New Pride took him to Philadelphia, as a project auditor for federal grant compliance for a hazardous waste cleanup site. Hard-core punk bands easily and often came to Philadelphia from New York and D.C., playing venues like Long March, Elk's Center, and Love Hall. Ken became intrigued by the cross-racial mix of young people engaged in the city's growing youth punk culture, with its rejection of the current values of society. Ken brings his empathy and non-judgmental appreciation to the struggles of this group of young characters who are choosing something like that second pathway of diminishing returns, above.

Ken may well have known about an early comment by playwright August Wilson, about learning to trust himself to not censor the conversational language that he was hearing and bringing into his plays. In *Black Punk* Ken follows suit.

BLACK PUNK

CAST

BP

LS – Alias "Lizard Spit," Alias Liz – He sometimes affects Black dialect and mannerisms

Sal – BP's Girlfriend and LS's first love

Marvin – a friend

Charles – a biker

"Frederick's of Hollywood"

A "Sloppy Drunk" Female

A "Woman in the Window"

SET: A Three-Dimensional Surreal Painting

At open, BP hangs on an upside-down cross. The lights are surreal, red. Music is heard in the background. BP gets off the cross aided by the Marvin and Charles who support it. BP calls to them.

BP

See we evolve or we devolve! *(They all laugh.)*

BP stands down center at an imaginary window facing the audience. He is extreme in appearance and dress – an affront to accepted values. At left is a graffiti ridden brick front and an upstairs window with a forlorn woman staring blankly.

BP's apartment is unlit in the background. Within the clutter there seems to be a human figure.

(Shouting, animated, angry)

> Derelict! Fuckin' derelict come peekin' in my window and then try to tell me what to do. What!? Well, kiss the crack in my raw ass *(He bends over and pulls down his pants)*. You like that? *(Pulls up pants.)* Yeah, I did it. If you don't like that, I got something else for you. *(Grabs "stuff")* Naw, slum scum, you started it. Did you come beggin' in my window? *(More agitated)* Naw, that's what I do to your Momma. *(Laughter in the background and then a pounding noise like a bass drum)*
>
> I wish you'd try it! *(Runs upstage and returns with a pitcher)* I'll douse yo' ass. *(Threatens to throw contents)* Naw, that's what you do to yo' Daddy. Yeah, you better take yo' raunchy ass somewhere else they don't want you. *(Pounding)*

How I look, that's my business. You worry 'bout cleanin' that vomit off your chest. Baptize you in yo' own filth. Been hangin' 'round here a thousan' years and goin' downhill like tomorrow don't matter. *(Laughter in the background.)* A brother can be anything he wants to be. I been where you ain't never goin' so you can't preach not one line a that brother ain't, brother cain't, brother gotta be shit to me. Yeah, leave. I'll run rings around your ass on any level you wanna deal. An' you only dealin' from the gutter right now so take a chill pill. I ain't got to go nowhere. You *(mocking)* 'unnerstan' that. You the one goin'. Come try to hang some shit on me an' ain't got a pot to piss in and barely got a dick to pee. I stepped away from that shit two ages ago. So, yo' Momma! Yo' Daddy! Yo' people feedin' worms! Yo' kids you ain't never gonna have. And your home boys and home girls dry fuckin' their lives away. Get out my face!

(Lights fade in upstage. More pounding. BP crosses upstage where LS sits. He is white and equally extreme, an affront befitting his character. He's dressed for winter.)

BP

(Still complaining)

Derelicts. I hate this first floor shit. You know what I mean? When I lived in the basement, it was just feet, legs and a peek at a twat or crotch every once in a while. Now you have your window open and they come up beggin' like you're a vendor or some shit. *(Pounding. BP mimics.)* 'Can I have a dime fo' some rot gut?'

LS

Move upstairs.

BP

Shit, might make me start actin' like that self-righteous son-of-a-bitch. *(Points at the ceiling)*

LS

Does he do that all the time?

BP

He's jealous 'cause I got a reason to make noise. When he's goin' off, I leave him be except... *(Crosses mischievously and extracts a broom handle from somewhere, topped with a huge brogan, work boot.)* ...every so often, I have to let his ass know I won't accept all his shit. You know what I mean. *(Posturing)* Can't dis' me every which way he wanna. *(LS laughs)* Should hear him show out when he's got some pink things up there. *(Squeals)* Shheee yii yii yiieee!

LS

(Laughs then joins the shouting)

Chaaaaos! Chaaos! Wanna go?

BP

Naw.

LS

Why not? C'mon. When's the last time we been there?

BP

Naw.

LS

(Flattering)

You radicalize the place, now you don't wanna go. C'mon.

BP

(Sits)

What place?

LS

What place? You know what place. Every place you be.

BP

So where I be?

LS

Here and now and anywhere you wanna be.

BP

Well, that's sure tellin' me. *(He laughs)*

LS

Chaos, that's where you be. So let's go. You game?

BP

Next time.

LS

What next time? There ain't no Chaos next time, there's Chaos now. C'mon, me an' you, BP and LS – Black Punk and Lizard Spit. *(Laughs uproariously)* Remember that? Yo' pizazz and my wacko, maniac sleeooze. *(Laughs)* We wore the place out.

BP

(Reflective)

Yeah, we did, didn't we?

LS

Well, time ain't wasted, just wastin', man.

BP

Not my agenda anymore.

LS

(Facetiously)

Agenda? What's that?

BP

You know what the fuck I'm sayin'.

LS

Okay, great! So what's your agenda now, man?

BP

No agenda.

LS

(Pauses to determine sincerity.)

Bullshit.

BP

Whatever.

LS

You don't give that up.

BP

I did.

LS

Why? Naw. Bullshit.

BP

Whatever.

LS

Okay. What?

BP

Are you listening?

LS

I don't know what it is. But you do. Gotta know.

BP

You're hanging stuff on me. The Messiah's come and gone.

LS

Naw, man, I'm just tryin' to figure it out. See, it ain't the edge. Everybody's got the edge. It's the jive and the surreal. That's what we got, man. Fused meaning.

BP

Bullshit!

LS

Okay, okay, no meaning. Hell, you know what I mean. – Something to latch onto. –Something more than…

BP

Nothin'.

LS

Brother sister stuff too? *(BP doesn't respond)* Right?

BP

What you know about brother, sister stuff? *(LS slaps hands "high five." BP laughs poignantly.)* Yeah, right.

Used to preach poetry. Used to call myself Black Vulcan, forging thoughts for Black minds.

I had a following of sorts. People wanna know what Black Vulcan was forgin' next. Near the end, I came before the people after a long time away and I said:

Black Vulcan!
Black Vulcan!
Forging thoughts for Black minds
And slack behinds. (He takes a long reflective pause.)
Has Black Vulcan been mumbling and rumbling in
The flaming bowels of the earth too long?
And no, I haven't forgotten Black Vulcan.
I carry his crimson sword through my heart;
Wrecked in luster
If not in spirit.
I am one withered hour past
"Free, [black], and twenty-one."
So now let Moses take my journey
For I have been to the mountain-top
And broken plaques;
I have been the tool and slave.
I have been proud Phoenix sifting ashes
And returned again as Cain.

LS

Sal digs that, right?

BP

Wrote about her before I met her:
Before rain,

Night clogs up clouds, full, low, bulbous,
Sagging darkly as a labored womb,
Until the midwife's prick
Delivers wailing pelts
To last long after gum wrappers
Have harbored about knees,
After that until came
A raven and a single twig from the trees.
I'd played Jason and Agamemnon,
Strutting in purple,
Fitted in silk.
She played the fleece and Mary and Joan
With golden hair
Flowing as purple waters majesty
Across the satin sheets on her bed.
Her tears of joy washed my feet.
She anointed me with scent full oils
Before the stake…
Before the flames…
Before the unwashed masses…
And clotting blood stains…
She was amazed when I recited for her. She's always sayin': 'Before you met me?' She can't believe it.

LS

She likes how you keep her guessin'.

BP

I don't try to keep her guessin'.

LS

I didn't say that. I mean, like the poems, you're sayin' something. She likes that.

BP

How do you know?

LS

(Self-consciously)

You know I know. But she knows me too well. *(Changing subject)* You do the "Kill Whitey Movement" thing?

BP

To the point of nearly getting killed.

LS

Great! Great! Tell it.

BP

Where's your gun?

LS

What?

BP

Your gun. Got to have your gun. You took the drama you're always tellin' me about. So get your gun.

LS

Skeezo! Skeezo! Okay, I got my gun. Liz got his gun.

BP

It was a time when ideals were real. If you had a message... *(Cueing LS)*

LS

You could speak it and...

BP

People would listen. If you had a... a blessed, pure thought, you could inherit... *(Cue)*

LS

...Inherit the Earth.

BP

And step before podiums, adjust mikes, and capture the minds and hearts of the masses. *(He pantomimes doing so.)* And capture their wrath. Shoot. *(BP poses elegantly. LS shoots. BP dies then rises.)* You could create or define righteous paths from ancient legacies and... Shoot! *(LS does a fancy roll and comes up shooting while on one knee. BP dies then rises, comes to a "podium" and "adjusts a mic.")* We had just finished a rally. I forget what it was for. Anyway, it was successful. Got attention. All sides were there. Right. Left. Far side. Two of our guys got jailed – good publicity. Jail was part of the bargain for the Vanguard. Then we hear rumors that there were explosives planted in the city jail. Heavy shit, right? It turned out it was real. The papers reported it. There was an explosion. But who did the planting? We honestly didn't know who could have done it. Was it a set up? Mysterious shit.

LS

(Impressed)

Really?

BP

Yeah. So, BOOM. Nobody killed or shit but a lotta people scared. Anyway, this was all learned later. Right then we were celebrating. Panamanian shit, 'shrooms, mes, zip yap speed and in a gada davida acid, man *(Laughs)*; free your mind, free your love connection. I swear, free love everywhere. *(Pause)* You know where I was?

LS

Where?

BP

I was under the kitchen table. It was draped with this lace I'll never forget. Draped all the way to the ground. Much better than this one. *(Indicates his floor length table cloth)*

LS

Drunk out of your mind, right?

BP

Not drunk. I was on an asteroid, man. I swear. *(LS laughs)* I was with this carmel sweet sister to beat all sisters under the table. Both of us in a multi-hued void on an asteroid small enough to see the curve of the horizon and jutting rocks and steamy mists fuming out of crap-colored pimples. And I was makin' James Brown proud.

LS

Yes, yes, the Godfather of soul bees…

BP

Talkin' with my body. Dancin' the camel walk. Yow!

LS

Eeeee Yow! Got-ta! Got-ta!

BP

Feelin' soul good with a hump in my back. *(Demonstrates sensually.)*

LS

(While performing a bastardized "James Brown" alternately with a hump in his back.)

Sheeeeeeuuu! Got-ta, got-ta, got-ta! James Brown. Put a hump in your back Sheee…

BP

Stop it!

LS

What?

BP

Just stop it. *(Changing subject)* Then boom! The door slams open. Pigs storm in shootin'.

LS

No jive?

BP

None whatsoever. Shoot. *(LS does so)* Down goes Clemett, who self-destiny had named Ahmad. He had hit a cop that day with a Pabst Blue Ribbon bottle. Ahmad fell and the blood oozed down his well-groomed Fu Manchu mustache, onto his black leather jacket, and then into a puddle inside his black leather Kango brim hat that looked like it was a serving bowl lying on the sofa. *(Sings gospel fashion)* The blood, the blood ohhh… Shoot! *(LS does)* Shoot! *(He does again)* Daryl and Darla once Winona were in the bedroom. She was stepping into the shower and he was lighting a reefer. Love musk and incense mixed with fire and brimstone. Daryl fell through the door. A dribble of sperm clotted on his thigh. The sister under the table with me was panicking royal. Her name was Belinda, no self-destiny for her. Self-destiny was ignored in the newspaper obituaries anyway. I muffled Belinda's panic screams as long as I could but she could not be contained. Would not be contained any longer. She crawled out from under the table. *(Pause)* Several days later, I came back to see a savage sister, supporter of her men, mistress of the vanguard reduced to her form drawn in chalk on the linoleum floor.

LS

Did you come out?

BP

(Shakes his head.)

I stayed there. I watched them round up the rest of the vanguard and take them out. Stayed there. Panic all around. The revolution live and uncompromising through the pattern of white lace.

LS

They didn't look? How long did you have to stay?

BP

They had to wrestle Terrence out. Brother was two hundred eighty pounds. Took all of 'em to kick his ass. So I was able to sneak out into the bedroom. Had to crawl over Darla, once Winona, blocking the window. They couldn't hear me over big brother Terrence's screams while they kicked his ass in the hallway.

LS

That's some shit.

BP

(Solemn)

They said the revolution would not be televised. But it was. A minute at six an' forty-five seconds at eleven.

Shoot. *(LS does so. BP dies and rises.)* So I stepped away. *(He steps away from the imaginary microphone.)*

LS

And here you are. *(They slap hands.)* Chaaoss! So you comin'?

BP

No haps.

LS

(Pissed)

Shit! Shit! Shit! (He sits silently for a moment then pulls out paraphernalia) Toot, pipe, or line? (He pulls out a twenty-dollar bill, coke pipe and syringe.)

BP

Toot. (LS passes the bill. BP begins searching for a mirror in one of the piles situated, almost surreally, throughout the room.)

LS

(As BP searches about the room.)

Some people are impressed when I do that.

BP
(Unconcerned)

Yeah?

LS

Not you though, huh?

BP
(Finds mirror and hands to LS.)

Why should I be?

LS
(Proudly)

See, that's what I mean. *(Takes out a vial.)* Please come with me.

BP

Where did you get this?

LS

A friend of Marvin's.

                          BP

Charles?

                          LS

Marvin and Charles don't...

                          BP

I know. So is it stash or market shit?

                          LS

Well, this is stash but I got some marketin' shit too. *(Semi-sarcastic)* You still make referrals, don't you?

                          BP

                      (Facetious)

You got it, pal-a-mine. *("Toots" a couple lines.)* Eee yi yi!

                          LS

          (Toots then stands suddenly.)

Yeahh! You know what else impresses 'em? It's when I look 'em in the eyes and I say: 'You wanna do me?' Say it sexy or matter of fact. And I don't give a shit what they say. 'You wanna do me?' They say yes and I say: 'How?' and I give 'em choices. Sexy or matter of fact. It wears 'em out. *(To BP)* Go ahead. I got all I want, right? *(BP toots)* Have you seen Sal?

BP

Have you?

LS

No. (He snorts)

BP

(Pushes him playfully. LS rolls over onto his back and opens his legs, knees up suggestively, playing a game.)

Bullshit.

LS
(Sexily)

You wanna do me?

BP

I want an answer.

LS

(Sitting on floor)

I haven't seen her. So you wanna do her?

BP

I've already done her, same as you.

LS

Dammit, man, you're always throwin' that up in my face.

BP

Your hang-up, not mine.

LS

No, it's yours 'cause you don't trust me.

BP

I don't have to trust either one of you. She's free, white and twenty-one. It's her body. She could give it to Pinocchio, Dumbo and the seven dwarfs. I don't give a shit.

LS

(Laughing)

Classic. Classic.

BP

I don't.

LS

Then why you been with her so long?

BP

You waitin' for me to leave?

LS

Dammit! See what I mean? Why you do me that way? I just asked why you been with her so long if you don't care.

BP

Just a matter of time.

LS

Okay. Well, with me it's just more. I mean we got emotional history, that's all.

                    BP

That's everything.

                    LS

Shit. It's nothing.

                    BP

Whatever.

                    LS

Look, we went to high school together. – Helped each other come out. You know what I mean?

                    BP

Please don't drag up that story again.

                    LS

You're the one doesn't understand.

                    BP

What's there to understand?

LS

Accept.

BP
(Annoyed)

I accept.

LS

It was a fuckin' phase, okay?

BP

You're damn right it was a 'fuckin' phase. *(LS realizes what he said. Both men laugh.)*

LS

I know I didn't tell you this story though.

BP

Okay, what?

LS
(Hyped)

Okay… Okay… Okay… Okay… *(Toots a line)* I was in the gym with all these guys, right? And I was tryin' not to look at their crotches. *(Toots a line)* And we're jazzin' each other about skid marks in the shorts and hair on the palms and mixin' sweat and Right Guard and somebody brings up fantasies 'cause it was brought up in Social Problems which included sex ed *(Is that a social problem?)* Anyway, everybody's tellin' along and getting' as graphic as you could in grunt terms, you know: 'I dreama boingin' a beautiful redhead on a boat to Hawaii while the sun is settin' an' shit. You know what I mean? So I blurt out: 'I fantasize bein' a babe, and before I know it, I'm 'fag', and 'homo' and 'dong butt' and I'm shouting my fantasy tryin' to help them see they don't understand but of course they don't give a shit anyway 'cause downin' me is so much fun. So, they're slappin' my ass and pokin' me with shoes and rolled up towels and shit while I explain. But they don't buy it. So I yell: 'No, listen, listen, I wanna be a babe with a guy's mind see 'cause girls can't just go around askin' for it. Right? Right? But I would and I wouldn't give a shit, right.' And finally, I got them to listen. 'Think about all the times and all the ways you wanted to boink some fine ass chick but you couldn't do it 'cause she wouldn't let you or you felt she wouldn't let you do it. But think, think if you was a babe with a boy's mind. You could do all the things you always wanted to do and wouldn't care about what anybody had to say.' So they came around.

(He sits on BP's lap.) And now I have exactly what I want. I go to Chaos and I can play… *(Performing)* Rudolph Valentino with an Arabian turban and silk crotch or I can be the queen bee bitch, tight ass, pink hair and spikes that won't quit. Yeah. Everybody loves it. I'm the Gospel of St. Liz.

BP

Domini. Domini.

LS

But not your agenda, right?

BP

Not my agenda.

LS
(Matter of factly)

Sure you don't wanna do me?

BP

Yes.

LS

Never?

BP

Never.

LS

Not your... 'agenda' or 'cause we're friends?

BP

What do you want?

LS

(Stands.)

Dammit! I just want you to come with me. Me and you make a new definition. Let's just do it!

(Shouts, stomps and then grabs the broom shoe and prepares to bang on the ceiling. BP catches the broom before he succeeds.)

Chaaaoss

(Both hold the broom handle. They "climb up" hand over hand. BP "tops" it. LS begs with his eyes. BP answers.)

BP

Go it alone tonight, bro. (Gestures as if masturbating. Lights begin to fade. We hear distant chanting against some relevant cause.)

LS

What's that?

BP

The college is up the street.

LS

Neighborhood's got it all, don't it?

BP

Yep.

LS

You can't keep it out, man. It'll come in sure as shit.

BP

It's already in.

LS

Well, let's go then. Quit bein' a fuckin' martyr for nothin'. Let's go.

BP

No haps.

Blackout except for the woman in the window. We hear a couple arguing over the chanting and a sorrowful crying over that. The crying remains as the lights fade up on BP and SAL. SAL is blonde and extreme in black. She sits on a kitchen table behind BP who leans on the table. SAL is crying on the back of BP's shoulder.

BP

Well, why did you go there then?

SAL

(Still crying)

Dammit, she's my mother for Christsake.

BP

Well, if you wanna keep goin' through this then it's your business.

SAL

(Still crying)

No, no, I've been there eight weeks, eight weeks and everything was okay, you know? But she never gives up.

BP

That's what I'm saying.

SAL

She makes me feel… Okay, here it is. I change my hair. She says – talking about her past as always – she says: "Well, dear, my hair shocked my parents as much as when I stopped eating meat. Pass the wild rice," she says. I tell her "I want meat, Mother. It's all dead whether it's green with chlorophyll or red with blood. It's dead!" And she agrees and I pass the wild rice. *(Cries)* I can't explain it.

BP

(Facing Sal)

It's okay. Forget it.

SAL

She thinks I'm an extension of her hippie fuck sixties! I keep telling her and telling her but she won't listen.

BP

Telling her what?

SAL

I just said it! I'm not an updated version of her.

BP

I understand.

SAL

No, you don't.

BP

OK, I don't. Whatever you want.

SAL

She even accepts me seeing you. Never met you but she's sure you're 'a heavy brother,' whatever the fuck that means to her. *(Pause)* I'm sorry. She just pisses me off.

BP

Obviously.

SAL

Okay here it is. Here it is. She insists… insists that I go with her. Where? To hold hands with her other lost in Hippie Zone friends with their long dresses and patched jeans. She wants me to play ring around a nuclear plant.

I try to make her understand, BP. I really try but she just takes my hand and kisses me, BP. Dammit, dammit, I try to make her understand.

BP

I believe you.

SAL

(Completely torn)

I even sang from Annihilation's first album. *(She sings in a tinny, pitiable voice)*:
Welcome nuclear flames
To blue skys clear
Turning all that's green
And living
To yellow death
Sands of oblivion
For only a minute of Eternity's
Day.
Oh, let me walk in
Annihilation's arms
Annihilation's kiss
Melting my skin
Rotting my bones
Blessed be the stalwart men
Wrapped in arms
Red with kisses
From blessed Annihilation
Blessed Annihilation…

So, anyway, she commends me on my voice. So, here I am. My mother's probably holding somebody's sweaty palms and singing or else she's on her fucking way to jail.

BP

(Wipes her tears.)

Have you been with anyone?

SAL

(Fragile)

No.

BP

(Kissing her)

You sure?

SAL

Yes.

BP

Did you wanna be with someone? (Kisses her. They move onto the table.)

SAL
No one except you.

BP
(Kissing)

That's what you tell 'em all. *(Lights fade)*

SAL
There is no all. (BP works buttons or ties. Blackout)

BP
Except LS.

SAL
Don't start.

BP
How do you work this?

SAL
I'll do it.

The woman in the window goes in while the light remains. Lights back up on BP. He sits on the table behind SAL. They are both partially wrapped in a blanket and are bare shouldered. MARVIN, wearing close cropped blonde hair, jeans with patches and plaid wool shirt, stands while he and SAL use a Ouija board. CHARLES, a biker and Marvin's friend, enters later.

MARVIN

'H-e-l-l'. I knew it. And he was a hell-raiser too. Got kilt between Morris Town and here. He'd had a babe and about a couple gallons of German beer direct from Frankburg. Well, almost direct.

SAL

Almost direct?

MARVIN

Yep. Morris Town is this German burg away from Germany. One third of the… oh, must be a population of about ninety-seven hunnert still speak only German while the rest of 'em's bi-lingual.

SAL

Nowadays?

MARVIN

You betcha. And in the USA of America. This friend of Charles' used to be part owner in a brewery over there.

He had all the equipment and the innards to make it over here.

ENTER CHARLES, big, burly and running. Immediately Marvin turns, upsetting the Ouija board.

CHARLES
Slaaaminn'! (He slams into Marvin. They slam each other throughout their dialogue.)

MARVIN
Fucker always tryin' to catch me by surprise.

CHARLES
I… I… I threw him into a pile of fifty slammers one time.

MARVIN
Flew in the air ten feet at least.

CHARLES
But they caught ya'.

MARVIN
Thank God.

CHARLES

(To BP)

So y'all talkin' *(Slam)* Talkin' 'bout Morris Town.

MARVIN

An' Billy and Denise livin' in Hell. (They both grunt and slam once more and then rest.)

CHARLES

(Panting to MARVIN)

Remember BP? *(To SAL)* Went into that town on his black alloy Harley…

MARVIN

Hunnert fifty bikes in one town.

CHARLES

Probably two hunnert seventy bikers, our vimens and the townies in that sparkling clean German town.

MARVIN

And not a Black brother in sight.

CHARLES

'Cept BP. Cocky and no fear.

MARVIN

About as scared as an elephant at a rabbit fight. *(They laugh.)*

CHARLES

(To SAL)

He the only reason we go to that fag joint now.

SAL

It isn't a fag joint.

CHARLES

It was till we started goin' there. 'Cause we don't go in no fag joints. *(They laugh.)*

MARVIN

No, we don't.

CHARLES

Now it's the slammin' joint. *(He slams Marvin)* Chaaoss!

MARVIN

(Slammin' back)

Chaaoss!

CHARLES

(Looking around)

Shit... you still got that leather coat. *(To SAL)* Had a leather coat with tails. You believe it. Classiest biker ever rode.

BP

It's somewhere.

CHARLES

For that matter, what you do with your bike?

BP

Sold it.

CHARLES

'Sold it?!' Your bike?!

SAL

I was with him when he did it.

MARVIN

So it's your fault.

SAL

No, I tried to talk him out of it. I usta love ridin' on the back of that thing. Especially at night. Time would disappear. The wind rushing in my ears and in my eyes was like a mist whizzing by. Oh, I loved it. We'd both wear black. Like shadows.

BP

Except her hair. Which almost got us killed. *(He laughs.)*

SAL

(Laughing)

Dude called me the 'nigger's witch while we were drivin' down the highway. BP jumped off the bike…

CHARLES

Kicked ass, didn't he? *(She nods.)* Never was scared to kick ass.

SAL

Ridin' like shadows…

BP

Feelin' the rumbling of that black machine between your thighs.

SAL

A streak of gold in the misty night.

MARVIN

There she go recitin'.

SAL

Yeah, right. Anyway, he sold it. I know he didn't get what it was worth. But I did.

BP

Yeah, she did, an' she still getting' it.

CHARLES

So who you sell it to? Bet I know him.

SAL

I doubt it.

BP

Sons of Darkness.

CHARLES

Black bikers.

SAL
(To BP)

Don't tell them.

MARVIN

Don't tell us what?

BP
(To SAL)

No matter.

SAL
(To CHARLES)

His favorite words now.

BP

Don't start.

SAL

He sold it. *(Long pause)* We were riding. It was two in the morning and I just didn't want BP to take me home. So we rode.

BP
(To CHARLES and MARVIN)

She gets that way.

MARVIN
(Joking)

Don't we know!

SAL

There was this little house with a porch way out back off the street. And there were a lot of bikes in the front yard.

So I said: 'Let's check it out, BP.' He didn't want to at first but he finally did. He used to do things to please me.

BP

I don't please you?

SAL

He'd do things like go places with me. When's the last time we went some damn place besides the land of squeals and moans?

CHARLES
(Laughing)

I like that. 'The land of squeals and moans', great.

SAL

That's what he calls it.

BP

You don't like it?

SAL

We walked through the bikes…

CHARLES

Great bikes?

SAL

Nothin' like BP's. Anyway, there was like a garden of weeds right by the house. It was all Black bikers...

CHARLES

And vimens?

SAL

Black 'vimens'. They stared me down like I was a raw sore but it seemed like it would be okay. I wasn't afraid because I was with BP.

BP

She was scared shitless. Damn near squeezed the blood out of my arm. *(She pulls BP up. They remain draped in the blanket.)*

SAL

The place was full of smoke. *('Smoke' begins to fill the room)* There was a red glow from a light in one of the corners of the room. *(Red light drenches the room from one of the surreal corners.)* We danced.

BP
(Dramatically)

And the people danced.

SAL
(To MARVIN and CHARLES)

Okay, dance.

MARVIN

How?

BP

Cool. A brother missing two front teeth, grease stains on his well-worn jeans but movin' mean and sure. *(MARVIN begins moving mean and sure with an imaginary partner.)* That's it. *(He dances awhile.)* Dancin' with your hands on an ass and legs poured into jeans so tight they looked painted on. They danced beside us. She turns toward me slow and weird with Red Sea eyes. Know what I mean?

CHARLES

Mary Jane eyes.

BP

Deep as they could be.

SAL

Their music. *(To CHARLES and MARVIN)* Keep dancin'. I couldn't get used to it at first. *(She dances a jerky dance. BP follows her while trying to keep the blanket on.)* BP kept sayin': 'Cool, baby, cool, cool, cool, baby.' Told me: Follow 'em, baby. Jerk and twist… 'the dance?' I said. 'No,' he said. 'The way'. So I watched. *(To MARVIN with the lady with the painted ass and red sea eyes and to CHARLES jerking and twisting but cool.)* Keep dancin'.

BP

(Sexily)

Cool, baby. That's it. Ride with it. Listen to your body. Ride it. Yeah, like that. Keep it right there. Right there.

SAL

I started getting it. Black bitches lookin' at me. Black dudes stealin' looks. Couldn't look directly 'cause of the women and because I was with BP.

CHARLES

(While still dancing)

Drinkin'?

SAL

To ease the tension. Lots of drinks to ease the tension. They had joints but wouldn't share none. I rolled my fuckin' own. *(Dancing alone in the blanket, her own sexy but not 'cool'.)* And I felt it. They began to disappear. I rode it. *(Lost in it.)* Mmmmmmmm, I rode it like it was supposed to be rode. I jerked it. SSSSS… I twisted it. I almost drai…nneeedd the muutherrr fuuuuckerrr… But then I bumped into one of… of…

BP

The sisters.

SAL

Fuckin' bitch. She pushed me. I told her I was sorry. Some guys stood up.

CHARLES

Awright! Gettin' ready to kick ass. *(He slams MARVIN.)*

SAL

The… sister grabbed me. She said: *(Mocked dialect)* 'You can kiss his ass or anything else he got. You can slink yo ass 'round here like a fuckin' whore but don't let it touch mine.' She said that. You believe it?

CHARLES

Kick ass! Kick ass! *(Slams MARVIN.)*

SAL

No, he called a cab. Made me wait in it outside. – Came and got in the cab. 'I sold the bike', he says and drives me home. *(They sit on the table. The mist begins to leave. The red light fades.)*

MARVIN

(After a pause)

Well, that's that.

CHARLES

Right. You know what we say about cowboys?

BP

What?

CHARLES

I read it in a john. Know why cowboys scratch their names on the inside of their belt buckles?

SAL

No, why?

CHARLES

So bikers will know who they're butt fuckin'. *(Everyone laughs.)*

MARVIN

Yeah, I saw that one. Where I saw it they spelled t-h-e-y'-r-e as t-h-e-r-e'. And then somebody had crossed it out and spelled t-h-i-e-r... *(They laugh.)* Wait, wait, somebody else had crossed that out and spelled t-h-e-i-r! *(They laugh.)* All of 'em a buncha dumb fucks. I love graffiti in the johns. Makes my shit happy.

CHARLES

Makes your asshole laugh eh, cowboy?

MARVIN

Fuck you. *(He slams him.)* Here's another one. It's really gross.

CHARLES

Tell it.

MARVIN

It's ethnic.

BP

Black?

MARVIN

No, Jewish.

CHARLES

Tell the sum bitch! *(Slams him.)*

MARVIN

Okay. Know why Jews wear those little beanies on their heads?

CHARLES

Hell no. Why?

MARVIN

So the Nazis could wipe their cocks off after a slurp job.

SAL

Gross. *(There's a long pause then finally)* Been here ever since. *(To BP.)* We never fought before.

BP

We don't fight now.

SAL

It's being here all the time.

BP

You gonna fight with me?

SAL

It's not the same.

BP

Here or somewhere else, I'm still me.

SAL

It's not the same. *(To CHARLES and MARVIN)* Let's do it. *(To BP)* Let's do it.

CHARLES

(To MARVIN)

That's our cue.

SAL

(Simulates dressing beneath the blanket then throws it to BP who remains shirtless.) When's the last time we dressed?

CHARLES

Ain't nothin' wrong with not dressin'.

SAL

(To CHARLES)

Let's go to Chaos.

CHARLES & MARVIN

Chaaoss!

SAL

C'mon, BP. Let's get the hell out. Put something on or don't put something on. Let's ride with Marvin and Charles.

CHARLES

Do some slammin'.

BP

Chaos.

SAL

Anywhere. Anywhere. We can just ride. Marvin, you know of places. Where could we go?

MARVIN

Hell, we been a lot of places. We could go to one of those or go to some new places.

SAL

What new places? *(He stammers.)* See, he knows of places. I'm sicka stayin' in here. I'm itchin' to move. You know how I get. Right, Charles?

CHARLES

Right. (He and MARVIN together while slammin'.) Chaaoss!! (Pounding from above.) Fuck you, son-of-a-bitch busy body got nothin' to do but stomp on the floor. (Crosses to the refrigerator and gets a beer, shakes it and sprays it at the ceiling before drinking.) Up yours, Buddy!! (Pounding)

MARVIN

Keep it up. You're gonna have the piglets up here in a minute.

CHARLES

Fuck 'em.

SAL

(Gathering items and putting them in a draw string bag while changing her clothes.)

Let's go. Don't look at me that way. I don't want any excuses. Get off the damn kitchen table.

(She pushes him. BP sits on the ground. Sal pushes him on his back and straddles him. CHARLES and MARVIN pretend to take seats and eat imaginary popcorn. CHARLES drinks his beer – "watching the show." SAL pounds on BP's chest and tickles him.)

You're comin' out with us, you beautiful black nigger. *(He grabs her hair. She kisses him.)* You're gonna take me anywhere I wanna go or anywhere you get the fancy, hear?

BP

I'm done with it.

SAL
(Tickling him)

I didn't hear you right. *(Kisses him.)* Did anybody hear him? See, nobody heard you. We're escaping this big closet, even if I have to pull you by your lip. *(Bites his bottom lip. She pulls him up, protesting.)*

BP
Quit. That hurts, *(Without anger)*, bitch. *(She let's go.)* Seriously, I'm not going.

SAL
I said I didn't hear that. *(She puts her hands in the back of his pants.)* Your black ass is going with me. *(Pleading)* I need you, BP. What the hell. Please? *(BP attempts an apologetic kiss. SAL slaps him and begins crying.)* Well, fuck you then. Just fuck you. *(She kicks MARVIN.)* Let's go. Get me the hell out of here. He ain't with us anymore.

(CHARLES and MARVIN cross to the door. BP sits on the table.)

BP
Are you coming back?

SAL
What the hell do you care?

BP

I asked you.

SAL

I can do what I damn well please. Go where I damn well please.

BP

I never said different.

SAL

Well, come with me. *(No answer.)* Well, stay here, bastard. Are you ashamed of me?

BP

Of course not.

SAL

Live our world but don't share yours?

BP

I don't have a fuckin' world!

SAL

You had it. You made it.

BP

Not my agenda anymore!

SAL

You sold your fuckin' bike! I'm sorry, BP. I'm sorry. *(Desperate)* I just can't stay here!

BP

Well, go to your Momma.

SAL

I'll go where I want. You don't tell me. And I'll see who I want whenever I want.

BP

You're free, white and twenty-one.

SAL

You're damn right. (SHE EXITS. CHARLES and MARVIN shrug apologetically then EXIT. BP climbs onto the kitchen table and sits with folded legs. Lights spot on him then up on the woman in the window. WE HEAR MUSIC as BP continues to sit. ENTER LS and an obviously homosexual male wearing tight leather pants with two oval cuts revealing his buttocks. Both men stand beside BP offering him a "toot, pipe or line." BP doesn't respond. THEY EXIT upstage, caressing. ENTER CHARLES and MARVIN with a SLOPPY DRUNK FEMALE. The three dance together, sharing a bottle and eventually EXIT upstage. The music continues. Then the group dance in and out of BP's light. MARVIN, CHARLES and the drunk EXIT. LS and his friend begin their EXIT. LS smacks his friend on the behind.)

LS

Frederick's of Hollywood. (They EXIT. ENTER CHARLES, MARVIN and SAL. The men stand by the door as they did on SAL's exit. SAL crosses to BP and slaps him then crosses to the door or exit area.)

SAL

You're damn right. (She EXITS. CHARLES and MARVIN shrug and then EXIT. ENTER LS into BP's light.)

LS
(Eerily)

You can't keep it out.

(MUSIC OUT. Both cross downstage to look out the "window.")

LS
(Making a deal)

Nothing matters anymore. Hey, don't worry, the worst that can happen is that you shoot the shit and it kills you, right? Best deal in town. A gift from the doomed.

BP

He's crazy.

LS

Wacko, bonkers, insane, profane, lame, maimed de-craned, refried, cranially mis-aligned, morosely…

BP

Enough's enough!

LS
(To someone outside)

You ever play the lottery? Me neither. But I was thinkin' about it. It's a matter of time. A person comes before you and picks a dud. Another comes and wins a lifetime prize. But nobody knows it until it's announced. In the limbo time between hope and winners, all the losers keep playin'. They don't know the winner's been played and they're destined to lose. They don't know that hope's in limbo. They just makin' that new hope, makin' that new dream somebody gonna get. They're that impossible in-between. So it's just a matter of time.

BP

(To someone outside)

Hey, and look, if you ever come knockin' on my window or peekin' in here tryin' to find this dude, or even walkin' past here too many times where I notice...

LS

He'll stomp your ass an' he don't play. Just see me when you see me. You too. Right. *(BP crosses upstage.)* You'll love it. *(The "person" leaves. LS remains.)* You should have come with me. *(Pause)* We went to Annihilation's concert. They jammed electric, man like you wouldn't believe. And they had everyone in their power, swaying to the beat. -Outdoor concert. The night I brought "Frederick's of Hollywood," remember? We screwed on a blanket, under the stars on the top of the hill behind the audience. One blanket over, they watched us. Two blankets over, we were stereo, homo hetero. I shared my needle that night. *(Crosses to BP)* Let me tell you something.

BP

Go ahead.

LS

What if I killed Sal?

BP

What are you on?

LS

Nothin'. It's a matter of time. Like you said but different. *(Laughs)* Time when you pop, time when you miss but don't know someone's popped and... Lord God please, please let it be in between. *(Pause)* There's another rally down the street. Booths and shit. People against everything. Your parents still alive?

BP

Yes.

LS

Mine too. Haven't seen them since Sal punked. *(Pause)* You?

BP

Letters once in a while.

LS

You ever do bourgeois?

BP

Lived bourgeois. *(Shrugs)* Ma and Pa had the moolah. *(Laughs)*

LS

Mine too, a little bit. *(Long pause)* Emotional history… She punked in Drama Class.

BP

I've heard it.

LS

Let me tell you again. *(Pause)* Great teacher. Brother. He was a real novelty at our school. Never told you that, right? Anyway, he had to have been a frustrated performer. It all came so easy to him and he gave it back to us so easy. Accepted so much of where we little shits must have been.

BP

I'm going to get a beer. *(Crosses)*

LS

You never want to hear it.

BP

I've heard it.

LS

She ran away.

BP

Dammit.

LS

The brother gave us an improv. Get this. Told us to be punkers at a formal ball. How did he know?

BP

Did he suggest because we were to be or were we to be because he suggested?

LS

Yes! Yes!

BP

No great trick.

LS

She ran away and then she came back after two weeks. Punked. Each time she ran, she came back. More punked. And he accepted her. She only came to his class. No others. Of course, you know she loved to read and recite…

BP

And the last time you met in a tree.

LS

Under a tree.

BP

Okay. Have you seen her?

LS

From the outside, you couldn't tell it was there. It was a big pine tree with sloping limbs. She had a bed-pallet and radio, junk food, pillow and everything. Said it was for when she got tired of crashin' with people.

BP

Dammit. Why do we have to go through this?

LS

(Begins crying.)

Because there ain't been nothin' like it since, asshole. I'm sorry, BP. Please forgive me.

BP

Forgive yourself, bastard. Upside down, outta mind, shit head.

LS

I'm sorry.

BP

(Softening)

C'mon, LS. You're making a big deal over nothin'.

LS

I don't know how it happened but…

BP

You fucked.

LS

Made love. Made love. First time for both of us. No one figured we were the big V. But we were. Joggers came by and a dog came in the middle of the mad moment. His master called him. "Come here, Pookie. Come here." We laughed and couldn't stop. It was all mixed together, the big C, the dog runnin' over us and everything all rolled up in a beautiful moment. You understand? I know she's yours, but...

BP

FUCK IT!

(LS EXITS crying which blends with SAL ENTERING, a mournful chorus.)

I'm glad to see you.

SAL
(Gaining control)

Are you?

BP

I said it.

SAL

(Crossing to him. He gets off the table and tries to kiss her but she stops him.)

Don't.

BP

Whatever.

SAL

No, not whatever!

BP

Okay. I don't want to fight. It's just been so long.

SAL

A lifetime.

BP

Don't go off.

SAL

Being me is not "going off."

BP

I didn't think you'd hold a grudge. I just didn't…

SAL

You just didn't! You just didn't!

BP

(Changing subject)

You stayed with your mother?

SAL

Sometimes. That's not it. *(She cries.)*

BP

Have you been with someone?

SAL

"Have I been with someone?!" "Have I been with someone?!" Do you always have to ask have…

                              BP

Fuckin' A right.

                              SAL

You don't care that I been with anybody.

                              BP

You're free…

                              SAL

You sound like a broken record. "Screech, stuck, screech, stuck, screech, stuck…"

                              BP

Leave then.

                              SAL

Love lines for the times: "Have you been with anyone?" But you don't fuckin' care except don't bring you anything you can't handle. I never ask you, BP. I never ask you.

                              BP

You don't have to.

SAL
(Hysterical)

Why not?!

BP

Because I fuckin' ask you.

SAL

I can lie.

BP

Why should you?

SAL

I never have. (BP reaches for her. She avoids him then crosses to the "window" and screams in tears.) LS HAS IT! DEMON'S GRIP! DEATH'S SPIT! JOY'S LAST LULLABY! (Now very quietly.) AIDS…

BP
(Stricken)

Were you with him?

SAL
(Fragile)

Yea. Satisfied?

BP

Oh, Sal!

SAL
(She hugs him.)

They said I don't have it. LS came to me to let me know. He cried like a baby for a day and a half. I fed him. He cried and let snot and slobber drip into his bowl and gave me names and numbers to call. *(In a monotone)* Simmons, 555-7984; Mary, 468-9112, Tommy 232-4949494949… I waited to check again and they still don't have it but… LS didn't even know he had the trait. He just decided to check one day and full blown, ain't been cared for, out of control, AIDS.

BP
(Distantly)

Just a matter of time. *(Pause)* You don't have it?

SAL

(Gets out the Ouija board.)

I fed him and read him a poem.

(BP sits on the table, SAL on the floor.)

(A lament) All in the land
The people sought the cultured ones
Rooted in their ancient ways.

(ENTER MARVIN to sit with Sal, hands on Ouija.)

It says I don't have it either.

MARVIN

Morrison? *(Pause)* Ha!

SAL

But they latched on and
Browned and dried up
Having pulled away from the ground.

CAST

Kill the past
To gain no future.
Who needs either anyway?

An evolutionary path
Requires an evolutionary commitment
The opposite
Leads an opposite way.
Become a shadow growth
Nurturing the cultured ones
Rooted in the ancient ways
Until they too
Pulled up
And stepped away…

(WILD MUSIC. BP's room becomes chaos. All but BP dance, interact, LEAVE, return. On three occasions, SAL slaps BP and repeats her EXIT. LS asks BP if he wants to do him then he lies atop SAL. He rolls off and she touches the Ouija.)

SAL

Marilyn?

(All but BP slam and yell. The knocking begins.)

ALL

Chaooss!

(They march Nazi fashion. Fall on each other. Cheer an imaginary band. "Fog" enters low to the ground. BP finally gets up and crosses absently through it all and retrieves the boot. We hear a distant rally of chanters against some relevant cause of the day. BP crosses extreme downstage and then to center. He pounds on the "ceiling." The sound is amplified. THE MEN AND

"DRUNK" HAVE EXITED. SAL now wears white with a red sash. THE MEN AND "DRUNK" RETURN with a cross. They strap BP to it with rope and stand him upside down. SAL kneels and cries beside the "DRUNK." The music crescendos. EXIT ALL. BP remains spotted. Slow fade to black on BP and the woman in the window.)

End of Play
No curtain call.

Continued Reading

For more fiction and poetry from author Ken Grimes, explore the tremendous range of topics of his writing in *Black Punk*'s companion book, *An Anthology from Another Bunch of Writers You Never Heard Of: The Humboldt Street Writers Group in Action.*

As a long-time group member, Ken served as key writing critic and coach. All the fiction and poetry he wrote during his final years is featured, including an autobiographical short story of his life's journey written from the viewpoint of his own body, right through his triumphs and deep into his battle with ALS.

BUSH LEAGUE BOOKS

www.ingramcontent.com/pod-product-compliance
Lightning Source LLC
Chambersburg PA
CBHW071728040426
42446CB00011B/2270